SWEEPING

SWEEPING UP THE HEART

A Father's Lament for His Daughter

Paul W. Nisly

Good Books

Intercourse, PA 17534

"Through Flood and Fire" appeared in partial form in *Best Sermons 4*, published by Harper Collins Publishers in 1991.

"Farm Widow" by William Jolliff first appeared in *The Shawnee Silhouette* (Spring, 1989). Reprinted by permission of William Jolliff.

The excerpt from *The Wounded Healer* by Henri Nouwen is reprinted by permission of Doubleday, a division of Bantam, Doubleday, Dell Publishing Group, Inc.

The excerpt from *Lament for a Son* by Nicholas Wolterstorff is reprinted by permission of Wm. B. Eerdmans Publishing Co.

All scripture quotations, unless indicated, are taken from the *Holy Bible, New International Version*. Copyright © 1973, 1978, 1984 International Bible Society. Used by permission of Zondervan Publishing House. All rights reserved.

The excerpt from *Too Early Frost* by Gerald Oosterveen © 1988 by Gerald Oosterveen is used by permission of the Zondervan Publishing House.

"The Minister," "In a Country Church," "The Belfry," and "In Church" all appear in *Poems of R.S. Thomas* © 1985. Used by permission of the University of Arkansas Press.

"The Widow's Lament in Springtime" by William Carlos Williams: *Collected Poems of William Carlos Williams, 1909-1939, Vol. 1.* Copyright 1938 by New Directions Publishing Corporation. Reprinted by permission of New Directions Publishing Corporation.

Excerpt from *Murder in the Cathedral* by T.S. Eliot © 1935, Harcourt, Brace, Jovanovich. Renewed in 1963 by T.S. Eliot. Reprinted by permission of the publisher.

From *The Power and the Glory* by Graham Greene. Copyright 1940, 1968 by Graham Greene. Used by permission of Viking Penguin, a division of Penguin Books, USA, Inc.

Excerpts from *Remembering*, copyright © 1988 by Wendell Berry. Published by North Point Press and reprinted by permission of Farrar, Straus & Giroux, Inc.

Excerpts from *A Prayer for Owen Meany*, copright © 1989 by Garp Enterprises, L. Reprinted by permission of William Morrow, Inc.

Acknowledgments

I am deeply grateful to Professor Ray M. Zercher and L. Lamar Nisly for their close reading of the manuscript and their extremely helpful suggestions.

Design by Dawn J. Ranck

Cover artwork, *"Evening Sky,"* a serigraph by David Peter Hunsberger

Library of Congress Cataloging-in-Publication Data
Nisly, Paul W.
    Sweeping up the heart : a father's lament for his daughter / Paul W. Nisly
        p. cm.
    ISBN: 1-56148-069-X (pbk.) : $6.95

    1. Grief—Religious aspects—Christianity. 2. Nisly, Janelle, d. 1987.
    3. Nisly, Paul W. I. Title.
BV4907.N57 1992
248.8'6—dc20   92-4565
                                                                                    CIP

Printed on recycled paper stock.

For Laura, Lamar and Randal,
who loved deeply

He passes through the swoop of the entrance ramp, and is at once hurtling along in four lanes of traffic that seems to have been speeding there forever. He speeds along with it, being careful, eternity gaping all around him. . . .

He is thinking about being careful, the bright crustaceans speeding all around him along the road, each enclosing its tender pulp of flesh, creatures of mud and light, each precious beyond telling for reasons never to be known to others . . . If one of those particles erred in flight, then an appalling innovation would occur, an entrance to another world mauled through the very air and light.

—*Wendell Berry, Remembering*

Many brave men lived before Agamemnon, but all are overwhelmed in unending night, unwept for, unknown, because they lack an inspired poet.

—*Horace, Odes*

Contents

Introduction

I have both dreaded and desired the task of offering these reflections. I desired the opportunity because as we have lived through these circumstances, we have searched to see how our experiences could offer support to others in similar situations. In some way, I believe, we have a need to validate our experiences, to demonstrate (to ourselves, at least) that all this pain has not been irrelevant and meaningless.

I wanted also the opportunity to bring tribute to our daughter. As I told our church congregation, if God had told me, "Paul, I'm going to let you choose the daughter you want," I could not have chosen better. She was all I could ever have desired in a daughter. Not perfect, of course—rather too much the perfectionist with herself and others—but a daughter so caring, so loyal, so altogether exceptional, that I count myself truly blessed.

But I dreaded the prospect of confronting the past two years with unblinking intensity. And I was overwhelmed with the task of trying to communicate something of the depth of these experiences. As I reflected and began to write, I scarcely found words for thought; much less did I have words adequate to convey to others some reasonable facsimile of the experience. A narrator in Faulkner's *Absalom, Absalom!* expresses the dilemma: "There are some things for which three words are three too many, and three thousand words that many too less, and this is one of them." My temptation was to sink into silence, acknowledging my inarticulateness as the only reasonable response in the face of great mystery.

I resist the temptation and offer these halting efforts. One never knows. The Spirit has powers we can only dimly imagine. May these words be quickened by the Spirit's breath.

— Paul W. Nisly

Spring, 1992

1.

The Truth is Bald and Cold

The academic dean announces each name with measured cadence. In response young men and women climb several steps, cross the stage with adult dignity and receive congratulations—and a diploma—from the college president. The scene is a familiar one, enacted in hundreds of small colleges across the country each year.

Why, then, on this bright May morning are the tears slipping down my cheeks—as I try unobtrusively to dry them? Rituals always provide opportunity for remembering, but this day brings more than the usual nostalgia. Today my daughter's presence seems almost palpable, an absence that is a presence.

Two years ago on this same stage, Janelle shyly, proudly received her diploma, a tangible—though rather inadequate—symbol of reward for her four years of dedicated effort as a nursing major. Four years of strenuous work, too-short nights, limited free time—and now public recognition of her achievements. Was the perfect 4.0 grade point average worth all the struggle, all the pain, I asked her after the ceremony. Her smile was full, her answer quick, "I think so. I wanted to do my best."

For many years her goal had been to enter the medical field, and now she had completed the first major step. Graduate school would no doubt come in a few years, but for now it was time to celebrate, time to rejoice. Some family members—an aunt and several cousins—had driven 1300 miles from Kansas, where most of our extended family lives, to join in the festive occasion.

Four months later, two weeks after she had begun working in a local hospital, her plans and dreams, our aspirations and fond desires, lay smashed in one wrenching of metal and hearts as a tractor-trailer rig failed to stop for a light, rear-ended several cars, and then crossed the median strip, crushing our daughter in her small car. Seat belts offer scant protection against tons of hurtling steel.

The facts now seem fairly simple: a driver was hurrying home; he failed to slow down adequately for the stoplight; and then he was unable to control his vehicle. But the rather ordinary "facts" of the case seem to have no clear linkage to the human dimensions of the situation.

On this late Friday afternoon, September 18, 1987, I was in my college office completing some administrative work when my wife, Laura, called with awful intensity in her voice, "Please come home right away. Pastor Sam is here, and he says Janelle has had a bad accident." One fears the worst—and absolutely denies that it could be possible.

Arriving home breathless after a dash on my bicycle, I found that no details were yet known except that the trauma nurse at the hospital had called with great urgency. We needed to make quick arrangements to let our two sons know where we were going (one was a student on the college campus, the other delivering papers). And then we rushed to the hospital, driving rapidly, defensively, knowing that we could cause another accident.

As I drove, I prayed more intensely than ever before in my forty-seven years. My wife and I joined our voices in spontaneous prayers torn from the heart. "Dear God, don't let it be too bad. Please, please work a miracle for her. Reach down your sovereign hand and touch Janelle." Impassioned, audible, short prayers. And I had a clear mental image—not a vision as such—but an image of a divine hand reaching down and touching her in her hospital bed.

At the emergency room the receptionist ushered us into a small room with only a few chairs. Her practiced response to our questions: "You will have to wait to see the doctor."

We waited for minutes—which seemed like hours—for the trauma nurse. "Is she still with us?" I asked urgently.

"She is right in the room next door."

"But what I mean is, is she still living?"

"The doctor will be here soon "—and my anxiety level multiplied. Still one hopes. After all, two of my sisters had been in serious vehicular accidents. They had had grievous injuries, and while they never fully recovered, they both lead productive lives.

Surely the doctor would report that the surgery was long and arduous, the risks for the future would be high, the recovery extended. But Janelle will survive—and eventually she will return to nearly her former strength. A limp, perhaps, which will be a difficulty for a nurse—but Janelle will cope. She has so much to offer—to her family, her profession, her church—and she's such a loyal daughter. She must recover—*will* recover.

The doctor, a young man, barely thirty, comes in, eyes brimming with unshed tears. "We did all we could."

"Do you mean she is really gone?"

"I'm afraid so. I'm very sorry."

We did all we could—words probably spoken in scores of trauma units daily—but they couldn't be spoken to us. And I, who am normally the emotional one in our family, couldn't even cry. As the nineteenth-century poet Emily Dickinson wrote,

> There is a pain—so utter—
> It swallows substance up—
> Then covers the Abyss with Trance—
> So Memory can step
> Around—across—upon it—
> As one within a Swoon—
> Goes safely—where an open eye—
> Would drop Him—Bone by Bone.
> —#599

I had no tears, just an absolute aching numbness. "May we go see her?"

"Yes, if you wish, but some people prefer to have their memories from before."

"Does she look really bad?" I had terrible visions of facial and scalp mutilation.

"No, it's not too bad," he reassured me.

We went in, the three of us, our son Lamar having now arrived with our pastor. There she lay on the cot, still beautiful, though with her eyes bruised and somewhat swollen. Her skin, already a little cool, was still soft and pliable. I kissed her cheek as I had so often in life. *Oh, Janelle, Janelle,* my only daughter, my gracious daughter. How I loved you.

But she who was always so responsive now lay quiet, silent—and cooling. Impossible. Utterly impossible.

As we stood by her side, I said, "The Lord could still perform a miracle. He raised people from the dead in the past." But with more realism I added, "Still I think if he were going to perform a miracle, he would have done it earlier."

And so perhaps an hour and a half after we first heard about the accident, we have confronted the worst we could imagine. Again in Emily Dickinson's words,

> The Truth, is Bald, and Cold—
> But that will hold—
> If any are not sure—
> We show them—prayer—
> But we, who know,
> Stop hoping, now—
> Looking at Death, is Dying—
> —#281

And so we died—a significant part of us—as we stood there helpless. Mother, father, middle brother (the younger brother to arrive later). We now knew—and stopped hoping.

2.

I Felt a Funeral in My Brain

I felt a Funeral, in my Brain,
And Mourners to and fro
Kept treading—treading—till it seemed
That sense was breaking through—

And when they all were seated,
A Service, like a Drum—
Kept beating—beating—till I thought
My Mind was going numb—
　　—E.D., #280

In sudden deaths the practical immediately crashes in on the surviving family members. A few minutes after we saw Janelle in the hospital room, and before the dreadful reality could fully assert itself in our minds, a crisp professional asked me to sign a release form for the body.

The *body!* It's my daughter—not a body. Yet is that figure now lying motionless on the hospital cot the essence of my daughter? Body and spirit form a living union—but if they are separated, what then?

But there is no time for theological or philosophical reflection. Decisions confront us almost instantly. "Do you know what funeral home you would like? We will make the appropriate contacts."

I am an ordained minister and have stood with families when they have lost elderly parents, or even middle-aged spouses. But I have never assisted someone in the church who suddenly lost a young son or daughter. Even if I had, I would never have been prepared for the shock of facing those decisions on what normally would have been an ordinary quiet Friday evening at the end of a busy week.

Now, suddenly, without hint, warning, or even premonition of danger, we have been thrust into the trauma of decision-making. How can I begin to think rationally? All I want to do is to hold my daughter as I did when she was small, to comfort her, to shield her, to restore her. But Janelle is beyond my feeble help.

Like Emily Dickinson, "I felt a Funeral, in my Brain/ . . . A Service, like a Drum—/ Kept beating—beating—till I thought/ My mind was going numb." In that numbness we returned home. How could I tell my next older sister 1300 miles away that our daughter, her niece, had been crushed under tons of mobile steel? Giving this message was unbearably painful, somewhat like examining one's arm which had been ripped from its socket, lifting it with the other trembling hand, and beginning to assess the devastating injury. Unreal. Completely incredible. Beyond words.

With "eternity gaping all around," our family entered into a world of grief and sorrow that we could not have imagined to exist. The carnage on American highways—45,000 *deaths* annually, plus thousands more *maimed*—has long seemed awful to me. But statistics do not begin to convey the mind-numbing loss of one flesh-and-blood daughter.

We are stunned, bewildered in our grief on this first night. Close friends come to be with us, to comfort us, to bring us food. But we cannot eat, nor will we be comforted. As the prophet said, "A voice is heard in Ramah, weeping and great mourning, Rachel weeping for her children and refusing to be comforted, because they are no more" (Matthew 2:18). That evening one dear friend said it even more succinctly, though less elegantly, when he groaned, "It stinks."

My wife and I sleep fitfully, wake, hold each other tightly, mingle our tears. The whole sequence of events lacks all semblance of ordinary reality: it can't be true, it isn't true; it *must not* be true. Janelle must be sleeping in her room—or perhaps she has gone on a trip, and her absence is only temporary. Time has stopped, yet the moments tick endlessly away until morning finally comes. Our lives, we are beginning to realize, have been irrevocably changed.

3.

The Solemnest of Industries

The Bustle in a House
The Morning after Death
Is solemnest of industries
Enacted upon Earth—

The sweeping up the Heart
And putting Love away
We shall not want to use again
Until Eternity.
—E.D., #1078

On Saturday morning we are thrust from the midnight of our souls to the blankness of a new day, a day marking the beginning of a new, stunning era in the life of our family.

Once again immediate decisions must be made as we prepare for the funeral. How can we bear to choose which of her dresses she will wear on this final public occasion? What dress would she choose, she who has always been so careful, so meticulous in her grooming? How can we face her closet, hung with clothing expressive of her tastes, her personality? It seems presumptuous that we would decide for our adult daughter, our oldest, what she should wear.

After making our decision, we go to the funeral home. The person in charge seems more than professional: he appears moved by the loss of one so young. We walk around the large room trying to pick out a casket which seems right for Janelle. The cheaper metal ones seem—well, cheap and crass. The hardwoods are beautiful—but appear over-priced.

As we wander around the room by ourselves, I remark to the others that one could believe we were on the set of a movie. The film would be titled "The Grieving Family" and would show middle-aged parents and their two sons trying to choose the appropriate casket. Surely, we were not doing this "for real," surely this charade must soon come to its conclusion, and then we will all step out of our acting roles and into our own characters. Everything will return to normal.

But decisions continued to press themselves upon us. Since we had moved to the area some fifteen years earlier, leaving our extended families in Kansas, we had not even considered buying burial lots. Now a lot must be chosen, quickly.

And an obituary must be prepared by 11:00 on this Saturday. More decisions need to be made: will there be a memorial fund? Where should it be established? What contacts need to be made to approve the college medical scholarship which we decided to initiate? What arrangements should be announced for the funeral at our church and the memorial service at the college?

Who will preach? Who will sing? What music will be played? The questions keep coming, for we want to plan a beautiful service for Janelle, who herself loved music and practiced the piano for many years. Overwhelmed as we are, how can we possibly make good decisions? Without experience, without preparation, we live a lifetime in a day, confronting decisions we never planned to make.

The "bustle in a house"—the "solemnest of industries"—does not for me include putting love away. But it does mean, particularly in an unforseen death, the need to decide quickly, without forethought or prior planning. And one feels unwilling—yes, completely incapable—of deciding. Yet needing to decide.

4.
Boots of Lead

And then I heard them lift a Box
And creak across my Soul
With those same Boots of Lead, again,
The Space—began to toll,

As all the Heavens were a Bell,
And Being, but an Ear,
And I, and Silence, some strange Race
Wrecked, solitary, here—
    —E.D., #209

On Tuesday morning, the day of public goodbyes, I awoke early and stood alone at our front door watching the changing sky. The day dawned brilliantly—incongruously so—but soon a small cloud passed over our village of Grantham, dropping a light shower. It seemed appropriate. The rain soon passed, but the weeping in my heart continued.

Before the service many people came to greet us, to hold us, to speak words of comfort. I was most moved by those who mingled their tears with ours. A dear brother-in-law came early. He seemed so sturdy and reliable, and yet so caring and broken that I sobbed in his strong arms. I felt purged, cleansed, strengthened. Then I could put on my more public face again.

The line stretches long, the funeral directors become uneasy, someone whispers in my ear, the pace quickens. We Westerners are driven by clocks: even our grief must fit schedules. The door is closed; only family and a few friends remain in the room. After the prayer by a minister friend, we gently, symbolically draw up the blanket around Janelle's shoulders—as we had done years earlier on cold winters' evenings.

We turn to enter the church sanctuary. In this public ceremony we reflect together, focusing on memories which have survived shattered glass and crumpled metal. "We are here to remember Janelle Nisly," our pastor says. "We are here to say goodbye, but also to say that we shall meet again. We are here to try to understand; we are here because we care. We are here to confront our own destiny." From Psalm 90 he reads, "Teach us to number our days aright, that we may gain a heart of wisdom." And so we look back on Janelle's too-short life.

Our deacon, who himself had lost his wife in middle-age, speaks of Janelle's radiant spirit, which will live on. He remarks on her willingness to serve, on her joy in encouraging others. He mentions her weekly bringing a freshly-baked coffee cake for her Sunday school class. Janelle was determined to do her part to give continuity and coherence to the College and Careers class.

A dear family friend recalls how our two families rejoiced together in good times and supported each other in hard times. She speaks of earlier occasions while our children were still young, when, after sharing a meal together, our children would go off to the basement, six children from two families, to make up a play. They would find suitable props, dress themselves in old clothes and, amidst great merriment, put on a show for their parents. Janelle enjoyed acting, loved friends, savored life.

One of Janelle's cousins, who filled an older sister role, speaks of the pleasure of watching her become a deeply committed, caring, sensitive young woman: "Janelle would often absorb the pain of other people, even when it meant that she would struggle and suffer because of it. She wanted to make her life all it could be."

But her cousin also recalls Janelle's contagious giggle and her eyes lighting up at someone's clever remark. She smiles through her tears as she recalls the spontaneous, rollicking laughter that filled the house when our two families were together.

Janelle's brother, just two and a half years younger, speaks of their childhood play, particularly while wearing doctor's and nurse's outfits, which their mother had made. He also remembers times when childish quarrels cropped up. From a note saved for perhaps fifteen years, he reads Janelle's word, "We should learn to fight not so much. We can do only with God's help." He remembers the two of them sitting on the swing set in our backyard and singing lustily for the entire neighborhood, "I've Been Redeemed."

He speaks of shared adolescent dreams, of adult conversations, of studying together in the college library. He mentions hours spent in practicing piano duets with his sister. Their last piece, "Eine Kleine Nachtmusik" will never be completed, though they had played part of it as an offertory in church only two weeks ago.

He reflects on her rock-solid family loyalty, her concern for each of its members, her sending notes of encouragement through the college campus mail system. Janelle's love flowed in a deep channel.

When it was my turn to speak, I said that I thought Janelle would have appreciated this beautiful service, the wonderful music, the great tributes, though she might have registered surprise. She certainly did not think of herself more highly than she ought; in fact, being a perfectionist, she was probably too hard on herself.

I took the audience back to a few selected days in Janelle's life. I spoke of the night twenty-one year's ago when Laura sat up in bed, saying, "I feel it coming," while I grabbed the alarm clock to time the intervals between pains. Early on a November morning, after a sleepless night, we were blessed with joy, Janelle Joy, our first-born, our much desired daughter. The junior and senior high school English classes may not have learned much from their first-year teacher on that Friday, but they saw a euphoric young man.

I recalled once giving Janelle a too-hard slap on the backside when she was about two. And I confessed how glad I was that I had thought about the incident and had apologized to Janelle within the last year, though she, of course, did not remember the earlier occasion.

Other days came to mind: her baptismal day at age twelve when she, alone in an instruction class, had made public her commitment to Christ, a faith which was often challenged but which continued to mature and deepen.

There was the July day in Europe when we were travelling by car through Germany. Her seven-year-old brother Randy needed to have a loose baby tooth pulled, but he didn't have enough courage to remove it himself. Patiently, Janelle wiggled and pushed until after hours of painstaking care, she finally succeeded. We always said she missed seeing Germany because of Randy's tooth.

In recent years one could most typically see Janelle curled in a favorite chair at home while reading or bent over her study desk writing or living in her library carrel at school. Always there seemed to be nursing modules to complete or patient's care plans to design or research work to be developed. We jokingly called the Nursing Department the "tree-killers" for their demanding paperwork load. But all of that work had come to an appropriate and rewarding climax on Graduation Day.

As I finished my comments, I leaned forward and pointed to the candles on the communion table. The flames were blowing in the fall breeze, the candles melting and burning too quickly. So, too, I said, Janelle's candle had burned brightly and now was snuffed out before anyone was ready.

The service ended, we began the walk to the adjacent cemetery. Often I have walked the same path to lay elderly parishioners to rest; never had the path seemed so long, so impossibly difficult. Boots of lead weighted our feet as we moved to the grim hole which was only partially masked by the phony green outdoor carpeting. In burying my child, I was burying part of myself. I am less than I was, less than I could have been.

Again, as on the day at the funeral home, there was at the graveside an air of unreality. This seemed like another set for a family movie, and we were again playing out our roles. But for this scene there were no rehearsals; there would be only one "take." And this cast included real parents and siblings with supporting family and friends. All the essential actors were there, including one who played a minor role. Somewhat to the side, a workman, leaning on a shovel and waiting for the committal service to be completed, seemed incongruous in this company of the grieving and well-dressed. He was simply doing his job, but he hadn't managed to move off-stage: now he was forever part of the memory film. Unreal reality.

> And then a Plank in Reason, broke,
> And I dropped down, and down—
> And hit a World, at every plunge,
> And Finished knowing—then—
> —E.D., #280

5.

The Feet,
Mechanical,
Go Round

After great pain, a formal feeling comes—
The Nerves sit ceremonious, like Tombs—
The stiff Heart questions was it He, that bore,
And Yesterday, or Centuries before?

The Feet, mechanical, go round—
Of Ground, or Air, or Ought—
A Wooden way
Regardless grown,
A Quartz contentment, like a stone—

This is the Hour of Lead—
Remember, if outlived,
As Freezing persons, recollect the Snow—
First—Chill—then Stupor—then the letting go—
    —E.D., #341

"Life goes on," the cliché has it. Yet when a family has been shattered by sudden death, everything seems to stop. Normal hunger pangs, sexual drives, ordinary sleeping patterns—nothing is "normal." Life *has* stopped for one—and for a time it seems to stop for others. Or at least one wishes that it would.

Janelle's accident occurred just a few weeks after the beginning of the fall term, a time when a heavy teaching load and much administrative work at the college, combined with church responsibilities, made my schedule full under the best of circumstances. How could one begin to function after the cataclysmic events of the past few days? A man whom I much respect said that for three weeks after the death of his son, he was simply prostrated, incapable of action. I, too, wanted to withdraw after the death of our daughter, yet the prospect of later returning to an even more daunting load made that course of action seem impossible. On Thursday two days after the funeral on Tuesday I received an urgent request from a college administrative office requiring my completion and submission of some forms by the beginning of the next week. No time to weep, no room to mourn.

The searing pain of the first days lessened, but I felt incredibly empty, hollow, drained. Why bother with the mundane, ordinary things which seemed of so little real import? I would listen to my colleagues' debate in committee or in the faculty business meeting and wonder whether these issues actually merited the time and energy we were giving them. Of what real significance was it whether we voted for this or that curricular option or administrative change? Would it make any ultimate difference? At one meeting I became particularly weary of the seemingly petty arguments, the apparent posturing. Compared with the ultimate issues of life and death, these details seemed insignificant. I thought of John M. Synge's Deirdre as she confronted the death of her husband: "Draw back awhile with the squabbling of fools." The significant and the trivial have a way of appearing in a new light when one faces the ancient enemy, death.

But these thoughts I do not speak to my colleagues. On most occasions I wear my public face. But actually we are the walking wounded, as I tell my wife. We move one foot in front of the other; we seem to be walking—but it cannot be described as ordinary locomotion. We move as in a dream, a trance, hoping that we will awaken and normality will return. Like wounded animals, already severely beaten, we hunker down, half expecting more blows. At the same time we go through the motions of ordinary life.

The weather that September and October seemed unusually beautiful—clear, brisk mornings, brilliant Kansas-blue skies with fluffy white clouds. Janelle would have loved it. But the natural beauty this fall seemed a sham, an external mockery which intensified the inner pain.

In some irrational way I thought that all "normal" activities should stop, or at least be severely curtailed. My office window is open to the fresh fall breeze, and I hear shouts at an athletic event, probably a soccer game. How can they be having fun as if nothing untoward had happened? I ride home on my bike, and a school bus stops in front of me unloading high school kids. As I wait in the street, several kids on the bus mock me through the open windows, calling me "old man." On another day I sit in the college dining hall eating lunch. Nearby a group of students is laughing raucously, repeatedly. How can people be so thoughtless?

Life should somehow stop for us—but it doesn't and we keep shuffling along. And confronting new pain. Insurance forms must be filled out, car titles signed over, the banking account clarified. I feel like an intruder; I, who have always honored our children's privacy, now find myself "prying" into our eldest's financial affairs. Are there any bills to be paid? Does she have savings? I find her bank passbook in her dresser drawer; I have never gone rummaging in her drawer before. It seems almost ghoulish.

Worst of all is sending copies of the death notice: to several insurance companies, to her hospital so her first paycheck can be released, to an airline so I can get a ticket to a literature conference changed. This is the hour of lead, unspeakably heavy.

For as long as I can remember the church has been an important part of our family's life, and friends have been wonderfully supportive. But Sundays in church are very difficult. Now there are only four seated in the pew where there should be five. Stanzas from familiar songs take on new meaning as we sing about the brevity and tenuousness of life and the inevitability of death. We sing about God's care for his children, and I wonder about his care for us when a simple divine action could have spared our daughter. We sing about God's love, and I reflect on a friend's comment after the sudden death of her husband: "If this [death] is an expression of God's love, then I wish he didn't love me so much."

Returning home after church—the four of us—how empty the house seems, how alone we feel without Janelle's presence and help. Sunday dinners were always special at our house, school and work laid aside, as we enjoyed being together. Now we try to cover the emptiness, the older son setting the table while I fry the meat and my wife prepares the salad. But our hearts know what we can't yet say: Janelle will never again be at our Sunday dinner.

As we go through the motions of living, I reflect that one of the most frustrating aspects of the entire experience has been my inability to *do* anything to change the situation. In Janelle's most critical need I could not do a thing. God knows I tried. How I cried out in prayer, how I sought divine inter-vention, how we longed for a miracle of healing. But her life had fled even as I was praying. "Multiple trauma" the death certificate said. How painfully true—multiple trauma—not only to Janelle, but to her parents, to her brothers, to the extended family and to her close friends. The trauma only began with the awful physical injuries.

We are the walking wounded. The feet, mechanical, go round.

6.

The Cry Stuck
in the Throat

But when you got up to go
There was a hand preventing you.
And when you tried to cry out, the cry got stuck
In your dry throat, and you lay there in travail,
Big with your cry, until dawn delivered you
And your cry was still-born and you arose and
     buried it,
Laying on it wreaths of the birds' songs,

But for some there is no dawn, only the light
Of the Cross burning up the long aisle
Of night; and for some there is not even that.
    —R. S. Thomas, "The Minister"

Is the Lord not in Zion?
Is her King no longer there?
    —Jeremiah 8:19

Death has climbed in through our windows
and has entered our fortresses;

> it has cut off the children from the streets
> and the young men from the public squares.
> —*Jeremiah 9:21*

Some months after the accident a minister and educator whom I respect greatly asked about our family. After some discussion he said that a friend of his remarked that one should never ask God why. Rather, one should ask, "What lessons can I learn from these events?" Perhaps. But the human questions still seem natural and honest—and not wrong—to me. As our deacon said to me on that first evening at the hospital, "We will be asking questions about this from here to eternity."

For me the critical question was not "Why us?" After all, some tens of thousands of people are killed on our nation's highways each year. My questions revolved around issues concerning God's nature. Where was God when these grotesque events took place? Why—if God is omnipotent—didn't he intervene? If God truly cares for his children, why didn't he rescue Janelle, who was dedicated to serving God through serving others? What is the nature of God's justice?

Not only were my questions about God troubling—and unanswered—but I confronted formidable questions about the nature and purpose of prayer. Does God hear prayer? If he hears, how does he respond? To the most urgent prayer in my life I had received a blank. Does prayer make—I mean *really* make—any difference?

"Give me a sign, God, a visible response. 'Oh that you would rend the heavens and come down, that the mountains would tremble before you!'" (Isaiah 64:1). But here the heavens didn't reveal a vision, nor were the mountains moved to the midst of the sea.

I had Job's questions, but lacked his courage as he shouted to God, "Why do you hide your face and consider me your enemy?" (Job 13:24). My belief in God was never in jeopardy. But the questions were, What *kind* of God do I serve? and, How can I *communicate* with him?

Job's question became my question.

I was, perhaps somewhat perversely, comforted by the soul-cries of the Psalmist:

> Awake, O Lord! Why do you sleep?
> Rouse yourself! Do not reject us forever.
> Why do you hide your face
> and forget our misery and oppression?
> —*Psalm 44:23-24*

Did I, like the 450 prophets of Baal, need to raise my voice to a shriek so that God could hear me? Had he gone on a journey? As R. S. Thomas, Welsh poet and Anglican priest, wrote in his poem "In a Country Church": "To one kneeling down no word came/ Only the wind's song, saddening the lips/ Of the grave saints, rigid in glass." Often in the past I had opened my college classes with prayer; now, while I still prayed privately, I became very chary of public prayers. In honesty I needed to be silent since God was silent with me. Words had lost their efficacy.

Again the tentative, searching voice of R. S. Thomas' poet-narrator spoke to me from his poem "In Church":

> Often I try
> To analyze the quality

Of its silences. Is this where God hides
From my searching? I have stopped to listen,
After the few people have gone,
To the air recomposing itself
For vigil. It has waited like this
Since the stones grouped themselves about it.
These are the hard ribs
Of a body that our prayers have failed
To animate.

◆ ◆ ◆

There is no other sound
In the darkness but the sound of a man
Breathing, testing his faith
On emptiness, nailing his questions
One by one to an untenanted cross.

Perhaps, if one were able to admit the naked truth, there
really is nothing that one can know beyond the silence, the
hiddenness of God. Or might the truth be worse? Suppose
the unnamed lieutenant in Graham Greene's *The Power and
the Glory* is credible in his skepticism: "They [the poor people]
deserved nothing less than the truth—a vacant universe and
a cooling world, the right to be happy in any way they chose."
If one could believe in a "vacant universe and a cooling
world," then possibly nothing at all would matter since the
core of everything would be a vast nothingness. *Nada* is small
comfort, of course, but at least one should not then be surprised at apparently meaningless death. But I cannot escape
through this route. I am both blessed and burdened with
belief in God which will not let me go; and thus I am pressed

back into the inescapable, awful mystery of life—and sudden death.

God is there, yes, but what God is this? The Whiskey Priest in Greene's novel says bitterly to the lieutenant,

> God *is* love. I don't say the heart doesn't feel a taste of it, but what a taste. The smallest glass of love mixed with a pint-pot of ditch-water. We wouldn't recognize *that* love. It might even look like hate. It would be enough to scare us—God's love. It set fire to a bush in the desert, didn't it, and smashed open graves and set the dead walking in the dark? Oh, a man like me would run a mile to get away if he felt that love around.

The prayers, the cries, are stuck in the throat, stillborn. Only in the Incarnation does there appear a light in the darkness, a glimmering of dawn. In Jesus, God did rend the heavens and come down—but not with the overwhelming power which we expected would set things right. This Jesus groans in agony of spirit, "My soul is overwhelmed with sorrow to the point of death. Stay here and keep watch with me." Beside this verse in my Bible I have written, "So true in extremity"—and dated it 9-18-87.

In my friend and colleague Ed Kuhlman's powerful book about his son Keith's illness and death, he quotes A. W. Tozer: "The man with the cross no longer controls his own destiny; he lost control when he picked up the cross. That cross immediately became to him an all-absorbing interest, an overwhelming interference." No longer in control of my destiny? I don't think I ever believed that I was fully in control. But one hopes for some sense of order, of reasonableness, of structure in life. One hopes not to be like a car careening down the side of a mountain—or a tractor-trailer rig smashing across a narrow median strip.

Yet our Lord himself apparently lost control. When in that most heart-wrenching cry in Scripture, indeed in all of literature, he laments, "My God, my God, why hast thou forsaken me?" he is no longer in control. Complete dependency, utter helplessness. Unlike an old or infirm person who loses control gradually, Jesus lost it all at once.

So did we.

What, then, shall I do as I lie prostrate on the ground? Deny God? Curse God and die? Three nights after the accident, I awoke from fitful sleep with Job's word on my lips, "Though he slay me, yet will I trust in him." The cry lodges in the heart.

7.

In Accidental Power

Apparently with no surprise
To any happy Flower
The Frost beheads it at its play—
In accidental power—
The blond Assassin passes on—
The Sun proceeds unmoved
To measure off another Day
For an Approving God.
    —E.D., #1624

There are times
When a black frost is upon
One's whole being, and the heart
In its bone belfry hangs and is dumb.
    —R. S. Thomas, "The Belfry"

On the day before the accident a chapel speaker at our
college used as his text the familiar words from Romans 8:28,
"For we know that all things work together for good to them
that love God, to them who are the called according to his
purpose." His was one of the best, most thoughtfully rea-

soned and balanced sermons which I have heard on the text. But later that day, when I met one of my classes, I reminded them that they should never use those familiar words as a club with which to beat the suffering into abject submission to God's sovereignty. Most people in pain, I added, don't want to hear about God's will. They want to be reassured that you care. Ironically, the following day I was thrust—our family was thrust—into the most all-consuming pain of our lives.

We had not exactly been strangers to difficulties. Sixteen years earlier, when I was in graduate school and we had two small children, my wife Laura began having very severe muscular and joint pains, pains which moved in leaps from one area of her body to another. After some considerable difficulty, the doctors diagnosed her problem as rheumatoid arthritis, a debilitating and crippling disease which today continues to be her constant companion and enemy, a Roger Chillingworth of the body.

Ten years later she discovered a suspicious lump in her breast; a biopsy and mastectomy followed in quick succession. And then she endured with considerable grace the enervating effects of chemotherapy treatments which brought her complete misery every three weeks for almost a year. Had our family not suffered enough? Was there no sense of fair play in the universe, no one to cry, "Halt, no more"? Could one only quiver, expecting a Cosmic Ironist to roll the dice once more?

Ironies abounded. Janelle had dedicated herself to serving others through the health-care profession. Now after two weeks in her first "real" job, her life had been extinguished. She went to Harrisburg Hospital early Friday morning, a strong, healthy, eager nurse; she returned to the hospital late

Friday afternoon, already dying.

Her orientation-work session had ended a little early on that Friday, and because of a sudden shower, a nursing friend offered her a ride to the parking lot. A minute or two made all the difference.

On every Friday afternoon the early weekend traffic was heavy. Janelle was always somewhat concerned with the rapidly moving vehicles at entrance and exit ramps near Harrisburg. But on this day she was only about a mile from home, having safely traversed the most dangerous sections. Janelle was a careful, defensive driver, one who avoided taking unnecessary risks. But tons of out-of-control diesel power left no escape route. There was no defense.

Perhaps a week after the accident, needing more thank you notes, I made a rather difficult trip to the funeral home—my first return. Leaving the building, I heard the loud squealing of tires nearby. A "hot" car with its young male driver was fishtailing away from the traffic light on Main Street, leaving behind two thin banners of smoky rubber. Why is the careful driver snuffed out, while the reckless one survives?

Janelle always had a strong desire for justice, both for herself and others. At times when she felt betrayed by an apparent injustice, I would try to give my support in whatever ways were possible. At other times when the situation seemed to me less critical, I would tease her, "Who said the world's fair?" But never before had anything in our lives seemed quite so unfair.

Is Someone watching? Does Someone care? Can Someone act? Or are events the result of "accidental power"? In his provocative book *Disappointment with God*, Philip Yancey writes perceptively, "No matter how we rationalize, God will sometimes *seem* unfair from the perspective of a person trapped in time." We see through a glass fogged by our individual perspectives, our limited perceptions. From my viewpoint, ironies seem much more apparent than satisfying answers. In bitter words William Percy (the novelist Walker Percy's uncle) writes, "The good die when they should live, the evil live when they should die; heroes perish and cowards escape, noble efforts do not succeed because they are noble, and wickedness is not consumed in its own nature."

We have heard friends of ours say that they can hardly wait for the day when their children are grown and leave the nest. While we knew that changes would inevitably, naturally come as children matured and later established their own families and careers, we savored our lives together as a family with three children growing up. We gardened together, we played Bali and Password, we regularly walked to the nearby Grantham Pond to enjoy picnics in the park, we worshiped together; in brief, we enjoyed each other. Now, with Emily Dickinson, it was hard not to feel "a Blame/ That Others could exist/ While She must finish quite" (#1100).

8.

The Cold Fire

The Widow's Lament in Springtime

Sorrow is my own yard
where the new grass
flames as it has flamed
often before but not
with the cold fire
that closes round me this year.
Thirtyfive years
I lived with my husband.
The plumtree is white today
with masses of flowers.
Masses of flowers
load the cherry branches
and color some bushes
yellow and some red
but the grief in my heart
is stronger than they
for though they were my joy
formerly, today I notice them
and turn away forgetting.

Today my son told me
that in the meadows,
at the edge of the heavy woods
in the distance, he saw
trees of white flowers.
I feel that I would like
to go there
and fall into those flowers
and sink into the marsh near them.
—*William Carlos Williams*

When someone you love dies, and you're not expecting it, you don't lose her all at once; you lose her in pieces over a long time—the way the mail stops coming, and her scent fades from the pillows and even from the clothes in her closet and drawers. Gradually, you accumulate the parts of her that are gone. Just when the day comes—when there's a particular missing part that overwhelms you with the feeling that she's gone, forever—there comes another day, and another specifically missing part.
—*John Irving, A Prayer for Owen Meany*

On November 5, Janelle's birthday, I wrote in my journal, "The day was gorgeous with beautiful blue skies, a brisk chill breeze—a Cathy Earnshaw day. But it was also World Communion Sunday, and the pain was a sullen throbbing in my side." No longer is there the wild grief of the first days. Now we face the bone-crunching, spirit-numbing awareness that there is no escape from the reality of death. Our lives were changed, forever, on one day.

I am moved by the power of T. S. Eliot's lines in *Murder in the Cathedral*:

> What day is the day that we
> know we hope for or fear for?
> Every day is the day we should
> fear from or hope from,
> One moment
> Weighs like another. Only in
> retrospection, selection,
> We say, that was the day. The
> critical moment
> That is always now, and here.

Since that day we have been freed from the hot, searing pain which had virtually immobilized us those first weeks. Now it was the dull ache of a long-festering wound which has healed poorly—though it has scabbed over—and which throbs each time one inadvertently bumps it. It's the ache of knowing that the *fact* of the case will never change, that always, always we will have a huge rent in the fabric of our family's life. Weeping or screaming—or mute resignation—nothing will change the awful fact.

We found there was nothing certain or programmatic about our grief. Elizabeth Kübler-Ross wrote about the several stages of grief: denial and isolation, anger, bargaining, depression, and, finally, acceptance. Her stages may offer some help—but they are too neat. For us there were no such clear stages, no definable categories. Grief was a *struggle*—some call it a journey—but if it is a journey, it's one with no clearly marked paths, no assured destination. Some have said that one needs a year to complete the journey, a year to pass through all the major family events: birthdays, anniversary, Christmas. My response to these events was unpredictable: the second Christmas was more difficult in some ways than the first, the third birthday more poignant than the second.

The pain comes without prior warning: a short student running a little hesitantly across campus looks from a distance exactly like your daughter; a young woman walking briskly in the street a half block in front of you has long, beautiful brown wavy hair like Janelle's; the teller in the bank reaches to take your check, and you notice that her fingers are long, straight, slender. With a stab of recognition you wonder whether she, too, plays the piano.

Grief is natural when we face any major loss, yet each death is unique. We are never left untouched; each death diminishes those left behind. When my mother died at age seventy-six after seventeen years of being an invalid or semi-invalid, our family was hardly surprised, but yet we mourned the loss of a loving, praying mother. Twelve years later when my father died at the full age of almost ninety-one, we had seen his increasing frailty, and yet I lamented the death of my last parent, a gentle, caring father. Although by this time I was middle-aged, I was not fully prepared to be without parents. But with the loss of my daughter, my world was turned upside-down, my life twisted more than I could have imagined.

In *Too Early Frost* Gerald Oosterveen writes with poignant power about the death of his oldest, a nine-year-old son. "It is unnatural," he writes. "One is not prepared for it. The death of a child tears apart a family like the uprooting of one plant out of a cluster that have been allowed to grow together in one pot. It cannot be done. All those roots become so intertwined over the years that nothing short of violence can separate them. And it leaves all the plants stunted."

There are perhaps special difficulties when one loses an adult child. The natural rhythms of the family, rhythms which have been developed through many years, are suddenly, irrevocably disrupted. Not only are there rhythms in the ways a family *does* things, but there are strong emotional expectations as well. Janelle was always the one who was most enthusiastic with the successes of others in the family; conversely, she was perhaps the most sensitive to other's feelings of hurt or discouragement. How can one cope with these losses? In *Death, Grief, and Mourning* G. Goner writes, "The most distressing and long-lasting of all griefs, it would seem, is that of the loss of a grown child. In such cases it seems to be literally true, and not just a figure of speech, that the parents never get over it."

The unnaturalness affects the remaining children as well. Some time after the accident my wife said to our older son, "You are now the oldest in the family." Immediately he responded, "Oh, no, Janelle is still the oldest." Was she? Obviously she was our firstborn, but now that she was no longer living, how did that affect our son's position? Was he still the middle child? After almost twenty years of knowing where he fit into the family configuration, the familiar, solid pentagon had collapsed into a wobbly rectangle. How will he begin to define his changed role? And will he and our younger son experience pressure to fill—in some way—the horrendous gap in our family's structure?

For all of us, special family occasions like birthdays and holidays became difficult. I resonate with John Irving's narrator in *A Prayer for Owen Meany*: "I have felt that the yuletide is a special hell for those families who have suffered any loss ... Christmas is our time to be aware of what we lack, of who's not home." One of our customs is to see lots of family slides on Christmas evening. Laura and I would have preferred skipping that part of our family's ritual on that first Christmas, but to our sons it was important to follow the usual pattern—so we did. For me the hardest part of the evening was seeing the visual record of who we had been. To see the infant, the toddler, the young child, the school-age girl—most of the slides were taken in the context of our family activities—was almost unbearably painful.

I found that my eyes were seeking Janelle in all the slides— looking for her quick smile or the set of her shoulders when she was miffed or the protective reach of her arms for her little brothers. It was Janelle I sought—the rest of us became background to the central subject. We have lots of family jokes, "inside" stories about the situations captured on the slides, and we each contribute our parts of the story. Together these bits of narrative become *our* story. How do we now tell the story?

As we watched, I silently reflected on the loneliness of grief. How could I know what my older son is thinking when he sees himself as a year-old toddler being "read" to by his big sister who was three? How fully could I enter into my younger son's emotions when he sees the three of them at his birthday dinner while he is blowing out the candles on the cake and Janelle is involuntarily pursing her lips? What does my wife experience when she sees pictures of herself pregnant, or later nursing her firstborn?

I think of a line from Virginia Woolf, "We perish, each alone." In some significant ways, we grieve, each alone. We share, yes, but at the core of our being, grief isolates. There are heart barriers which we cannot finally cross. Is loneliness the quintessential aspect of our humanness? The cold fire of grief burns in each soul, individually.

9.

Foolishness about Lovers Dying

Farm Widow

She stands in his sheep barn,
where the smells of wool and urine
have not and will never go away,
but will stay in the wood of the beams
and the cracked concrete of the floor
until her sons tear the barn down,
and ever after,
people driving by will say,
"That was Elmer's sheep barn, there."

She, Elmer's old woman,
will be dead by then,
would be dead now if she had her way:
She has come to the barn to cry.
At noon she went to the cellar and found
a can of berries that he'd picked.
She smiled, and could not eat them,
and she cried and retched,

then came into the sheep barn.

She knows well that people
who write songs and TV shows
and such foolishness about lovers dying
are liars, that it's not beautiful
like they make it out to be, not at all.
It hurts until you don't even know
if the fifty-three years you had
together, though they were pretty good,
pretty much, were worth—this.
　　　　—*William Jolliff*

The death, then, of a beautiful woman is,
unquestionably, the most poetical topic in the world.
　　　　—*Edgar Allan Poe, "The Philosophy of Composition"*

Because death is such a pivotal event in human affairs, it
often becomes the theme of writers and other artists. But
there is always the temptation to sentimentalize—or mini-
malize—the hardness of death. In Walt Whitman's long
poem, "Out of the Cradle Endlessly Rocking," he writes
about death:

Whereto answering, the sea,
Delaying not, hurrying not,
Whisper'd me through the night, and very plainly
　　　before daybreak,
Lisp'd to me the low and delicious word death,
And again death, death, death, death . . .

But the actual death of a beautiful young woman does not

whisper, nor is the word "death" delicious: it is hard and cold as steel in winter. For months I could not even utter the word "death" in connection with my daughter.

Death is an enemy; death marks an end; death means we are no longer in control. As a former student remarked in her letter, at the death of someone close to us, we must admit that we have been defeated. Such defeat seems particularly painful to me as a father who wants to protect, defend his children. And at this most critical juncture I was totally powerless to help. Death means the loss of control.

The death of the young also means the loss of the future, the hopes, the plans, the dreams. Perhaps Janelle would have continued in hospital nursing, or she might have gone on to medical school, or most likely she would have taken graduate degrees and returned to academia. The world lay open with many possibilities—but now the future of service was gone.

For the family there is also the loss of the next generation. I used to tease my kids, "Don't forget that we want grandchildren." But for Janelle there will be no children.

Personally, I lost a daughter who was for me the embodiment of caring, of support, of loving response. Often she sent notes to me through campus mail, sometimes about struggles she was having, sometimes about problems she knew I was facing.

Once when I was getting ready to leave campus for a committee meeting, she wrote the following:

> Dear Dad, ("Number one")!
>   Hope this note gets to you before you leave for Wash., D.C., but ya never know with C/M! Anyway I hope you have/had (circle one) a very good trip and a very

profitable, beneficial, worthwhile meeting (I felt redundant!).

Don't get mugged, lost, hooked on drugs or become involved with any of the other evils of the big bad world in the city.

> *You are loved,*
> Janelle

Always she was sensitive to others who were experiencing loss and hurts, sometimes herself carrying a heavy burden for others. She grieved for a student who had an alcoholic, abusive father; she suffered with the friend who seemed to be developing a serious physical problem. To me she wrote after the death of my father (in 1984):

Dear Dad,

I wanted to write a note all last week and never managed to get around to it. I just wanted to let you know that in this time of memories of Granddaddy that I've been praying for you as you relive the loss.

I'm glad you have good memories despite of what most people would consider horrible abuse of the child labor laws [referring to my early work on our farm] and after that simply too much responsibility for one young man. I appreciate all you've done for me as well as for the family. Thanks for your strong marriage despite all the difficulties you and Mom have faced.

> *Liebe,*
> Janelle

To a fellow nursing student she wrote:

>*Dear _____,*
>
>*In reflecting on our talk this afternoon, I was sitting here this evening doing the inevitable—care plans, and I happened to glance up and saw this little tattered and torn statement I have above my desk. I try to read it frequently because I'm so guilty of not forgiving myself.*
>
>*I want to share it with you. "Be gentle with yourself, learn to love yourself, for only as we have the right attitudes towards ourselves can we have the right attitudes towards others." Wilifred Peterson*
>
>*I hope it helps you as you work through some of your inner struggle. I sense that this is an incredibly rough time in your life. May God send you his peace in dealing with this.*
>
>>*Shalom,*
>>Janelle

As her note to her friend may suggest, Janelle was a perfectionist who expected much of herself. Sometimes she placed impossible demands on herself and consequently faced discouragement.

>*To my good Papa:*
>
>*Thanks a million for the letter I received on Mon. . . . I appreciate (more than words can express) your support. I am not always able to look in the mirror and see those qualities which you mentioned. Actually, it is often rather difficult to see them, although at times I am able to see glimmers.*

I hope your sessions go well with your interviewee . . . Also I want to let you know that you'll be in my thoughts and prayers for the Mon. faculty meeting. Goodness, you probably need a double dose of powdermilk biscuits and Raw Bits! . . . [references to the "Prairie Home Companion" radio show, a family favorite].

> Love,
> Janelle

Another time she wrote after a struggle in a course:

Papa,

Thanks a lot for listening to me the other day. I hope you weren't late to your meeting. I know I have people cheering me on and praying for me, but it's awfully hard when you "fail" time after time [a reference to a possible "B" in the course].

Well, back to studying.

> *Liebe,*
> Deine Tochter

P.S. Have a super time at the F.O. [Flannery O'Connor] conference. I hope people show—it should be great.

Even when things in her life were difficult, she had the sensitivity to remember the needs and joys of others. But in one ripping of metal and flesh all notes ceased. Offer me no foolishness about the beauty of a daughter's death.

10.

To Cure this Deadly Grief?

Shards

The jagged shards
of yesterday
tucked away
in the
rag bag of my memories
are sharp
today as ever.

And every time
I rummage there
I bleed again
though
there are soft things
too.

—*Gerald Oosterveen,*
Too Early Frost

In Shakespeare's *Macbeth* after the murder of Macduff's family, we hear the following anguished dialogue.

Malcolm: Be comforted.
Let's make us med'cines of our great revenge,
To cure this deadly grief.

Macduff: He has no children.—All my pretty ones?
Did you say all? O hell-kite! All?
What, all my pretty chickens and their dam
At one fell swoop?

Malcolm: Dispute it like a man.

Macduff: I shall do so;
But I must also feel it as a man.
I cannot but remember such things were
That were most precious to me. Did heaven
look on,
And would not take their part?

In Joseph Conrad's novel *Victory*, the remote, isolated island home of a man and woman is being invaded by a trio of desperados. Realizing their danger, Lena says to her companion, "It's perhaps in trouble that people get to know each other." Her comment seems to me profoundly true. The sterling character of many, the alloy of a few, shines through as they meet others in difficulty.

Often I have been grateful that my wife and I can enter deeply into each other's pain. Yet we also need the help and understanding of others; in times of cataclysmic upheaval our own resources are limited. If I am bent double in agony, how can I adequately support my wife who is also collapsing? How, on the other hand, will she marshall the necessary strength to undergird me in my weakness?

Thank God for those who stood with us, who strengthened us during these times. Two cousins whom I had not seen for years, two days after the accident travelled almost four hours to be with us for several hours—eight total hours of travel on a Sunday afternoon and night to offer us their presence and love. On a Friday afternoon, exactly a week after the accident, I finished teaching a class and turned to leave, thinking I had hidden my feelings rather well. A young woman hesitated until most of the other students had left and then startled me: "I just want to give you a hug."

Many students, especially women, sent notes for weeks after the accident. One wrote to me, "This is just a little note letting you know that someone is thinking of and praying for you today. I realize that the weekends are tough for you and your family, but I just want you to know that I care and I still cry for you and your pain. Even though I cannot fully understand your pain, I just wanted to tell you that I care."

At times I felt an incredible emptiness as if there were an actual physical void in my body. On one such occasion I returned to my office after teaching a class which seemed uncharacteristically dull and unresponsive. The well of my emotional resources was drained, seemingly depleted. Later that forenoon a former student, now a secretary, came to my office, saying, "I came to give you a hug." The human touch heals, restores.

A good friend and colleague stopped in the hallway on another occasion to offer me his concern. "When I walk past your house," he said, "I think of an empty room, an empty chair, empty hearts." I am humbled and encouraged by his thoughtfulness. Grief shared becomes more bearable.

You continue to grieve but as the weeks and months pass, you think perhaps you should say less about your own feelings. After all, others do need to get on with their lives; what right do you have to impose pain on them? And some appear to forget quickly.

Others seem to want *us* to forget, too, or assume that we don't want to be reminded. What those without the experience cannot imagine is what a towering preoccupation the death of one's child becomes. Forget! For months in any vacant moment, thoughts of my daughter would rush in. We cannot forget—nor do we want to, were it possible. Rather, those who are grieving need to be permitted—yes, encouraged—to remember. As Abraham Schmitt says in his helpful book *Turn Again to Life*, "Tomorrow will not be better for the grieving ones as long as they meet persons who continue to say . . . [that it will]."

But what a wonderful gift when others remember. Exactly six months after the accident a dear family friend said, "Today is six months, isn't it?" Moved by her thoughtfulness, I could barely nod my answer. "I want you to know," she continued, "that I have prayed for you every day." I am left dumb in the presence of such caring, such generosity of spirit.

There are no simple, formulaic solutions to cure grief, no quick fixes for the anguished spirit. About nine months after the accident, as we were visiting another church, a longtime acquaintance asked me, "Well, are things pretty well back to normal?" I could have collapsed on the floor, but with Germanic reserve I murmured that, no, life was not "normal."

Not long before that we were arranging to leave on our annual trip from Pennsylvania to visit family and friends in Kansas, our parental home. On the evening when we were loading the car in preparation for an early-morning departure, I became almost dysfunctional. Somehow trying to get the clothing and other luggage loaded became so overwhelmingly, unbearably grief-producing that I found it almost impossible to complete these routine tasks.

Of all the family Janelle was perhaps the one most excited about our annual pilgrimage to Kansas. For her the extended family was very important, and a few of the cousins were almost like sisters to her. Trying now to get ready to leave was again ripping, clawing the scabs from the wounds, injuries which had seemed somewhat healed.

Because we have travelled the road to Kansas so often, there are a number of things which we always do: certain restaurants where we eat, an ice cream shop in Missouri which we seek, motels where we stay. Do we follow the routines from the past? Do we deliberately avoid the associations?

Arriving finally at my in-laws, I was physically bone-weary and psychologically depleted. As we sat down to eat dinner with Laura's family, the pain of Janelle's absence—her quick smile, her ready giggle, her pleasure in being with family—was almost unbearable. Inwardly torn, I could have turned and headed back to Pennsylvania again. We stayed, of course, but each time we entered a sibling's home during our visit, Janelle's *absence* was as vivid as her presence in the past. Life was not "pretty well back to normal again."

Most of our friends in Kansas and elsewhere did not try to explain why the events of September 18 took place. A few, trying to help, did attempt explanations—or asked thoughtless questions. One medical doctor, not from our church, had the temerity to ask what was Janelle's *spiritual* condition. I was, frankly, outraged. Had she not been a deeply committed believer, what would his question have served except to bring more pain to the parents? Could he hope to change her eternal destiny now?

Another acquaintance, a minister, said that while he would not apply his words to our case, he had found that when people became too comfortable, God often sent hard things into their lives to make them realize their dependence on God. He repeated his statement for emphasis. Although I swallowed my words, I wanted to shout that my wife's rheumatoid arthritis, her several major surgeries and devastating chemotherapy treatments would have seemed adequate to keep us from being "too comfortable."

A relative of ours, well-meaning, I'm sure, said she was confident that God never made any mistakes. My lips were sealed, or I might have blurted out that I didn't know much about *God's* way, but that I was certain that truck drivers made mistakes. And I wasn't sure that we should blame God for the incompetence of a truck driver who lost control of his vehicle.

Our relative also said that it seemed God often chose the *elite* among his children, his very special ones, to call home to heaven. God calls home the specially gifted, she said, the unusually committed. To me these attempts to comfort us fell flat, but then I'm never sure how these theodicies are supposed to work out.

I recall that at the funeral for my nine-month-old nephew, the minister said that although some people need sixty, seventy, even eighty years to live out their lives, some do it more rapidly. This little fellow, he said, pointing to the coffin, had completed everything he needed to do in his lifetime in a mere nine months. Nothing was left undone; he needed no more time. Perhaps some found comfort in his words. For me, silence would have been preferable.

I know of no cures for grief, no explanations which will mitigate the loss. But in the presence of people who love us, we begin to recover hope in the midst of pain. "Explanations" I find useless—worse than useless—for they often inflict further injury. But the word of love, the encouraging hug, in these God's presence is made real.

In the abyss of grief we recognize our vulnerability, our precarious grasp on life itself. At the funeral a minister friend told me that the word which kept coming to him was that Jesus is our rock, our firm place to stand. I appreciate and believe that word, but I probably shocked my friend when I said that at the moment the rock seemed quite slippery. What is to keep us, I thought to myself, from smashing on the boulders beneath?

And, indeed, life did not seem to stabilize. Six months after the accident one of our sons came to our bedroom door early on a Sunday morning. He waved his arms and made a gurgling sound, and on the instant of awakening, I thought it was our younger son needing to regurgitate. Jumping up, I steered him in the darkness to the bathroom, and discovered by the night-light that it was our older son. He pointed to his throat, and suddenly his agony came crashing into my consciousness: he was choking. Desperately, Laura called 911 for the ambulance. We were completely frantic. I asked my son what I should do but, as I realized later, he could not speak. One's mind races madly in such circumstances. I could already see myself making a second tearful call to my sister, later receiving the outpouring of sympathy from friends. But I didn't want sympathy—I wanted my son. Those eternal wretched moments were unmitigated horror.

Providentially, I gained the presence of mind to try the

Heimlich maneuver on him, and he immediately began to cough. Later we were shocked to hear that Lamar has no memory of my doing the maneuver; he had partially lost consciousness already. Words only begin to convey the trauma of those short, lifelong moments.

Later at the emergency room the doctor diagnosed him as having tracheo-bronchitis. Heavy phlegm had apparently cut off the air passage, leading to the choking. Lamar had subsequent nighttime attacks, but none were so alarmingly threatening as was the first.

In my value structure, family ranks quite high. Take away my job, my status, my security—but please, dear God, leave my family intact. Now we had lost our firstborn, and the prospect of something dreadful happening to our second was so awful that even now writing about the experience is difficult. At the time I felt that one more trauma would push me over the cliff emotionally. Jane Bernstein puts the matter clearly: "Grief makes us aware how fragile we are, how powerless to determine our own fate. It is not like chicken pox, with guaranteed immunity after one bad case. No matter what happened in the past, something worse can happen in the future" *(Loving Rachel)*.

And Christians appear to be as vulnerable as non-Christians.

11.

Through Flood
and Fire

Psalm 88: On the Brink of Despair

O Lord, the God who saves me,
    day and night I cry out before you.

May my prayer come before you;
    turn your ear to my cry.

For my soul is full of trouble
    and my life draws near the grave.
I am counted among those who go
    down to the pit;
I am like a man without strength.
    I am set apart with the dead,
        like the slain who lie in the grave,
    whom you remember no more,
        who are cut off from your care.

You have put me in the lowest pit,
    in the darkest depths.

Your wrath lies heavily upon me;
>   you have overwhelmed me with all
>   your waves.
You have taken from me my closest
>   friends
>   and have made me repulsive to
>   them.
I am confined and cannot escape;
>   my eyes are dim with grief.

I call to you, O Lord, every day;
>   I spread out my hands to you.
Do you show your wonders to the
>   dead?
>   Do those who are dead rise up and
>   praise you?
Is your love declared in the grave,
>   your faithfulness in Destruction?

♦ ♦ ♦

But I cry to you for help, O Lord;
>   in the morning my prayer comes
>   before you.
Why, O Lord, do you reject me
>   and hide your face from me?

Your wrath has swept over me;
>   your terrors have destroyed me.
All day long they surround me like a
>   flood;
>   they have completely engulfed me.
You have taken my companions and

loved ones from me;
the darkness is my closest friend.

Isaiah 43: A Word of Hope

But now, this is what the Lord says—
he who created you, O Jacob,
he who formed you, O Israel:
"Fear not, for I have redeemed you;
I have called you by name; you are mine.
When you pass through the waters,
    I will be with you;
and when you pass through the rivers,
    they will not sweep over you.
When you walk through the fire,
    you will not be burned;
    the flames will not set you ablaze.
For I am the Lord, your God,
    the Holy One of Israel, your Savior."

Until a person experiences suffering,
he cannot know what it means to hope.
—*Martin Luther*

God weeps with us so that one day
we may laugh with him.
—*Jürgen Moltman*

In the weeks and months following the accident, I have

continued to puzzle over some of the theological dimensions of suffering and loss. The problem of suffering and the believer is at least as old as the book of Job. The questions raised are vexingly complex, and no answers seem to be entirely satisfying, particularly for those who find themselves in the throes of suffering. Indeed, each person seems forced to come to individual solutions, to write his or her own book, as it were. Some thoughts in process are the best I can offer on the ageless dilemma of suffering in a world where God is supposed to be in charge.

Three simple questions focus my reflections as they have evolved in these months:

1. Should believers suffer?
2. Where is God when we suffer?
3. Why does God suffer?

Should Believers Suffer?

Some Christians—especially in North America—seem to think the answer is "no." If we have the needed level of commitment to Jesus Christ, and if we have faith as we ought, then we will not suffer. God is our heavenly parent, the reasoning goes, and if earthly mothers and fathers want good for their children, surely God wants better for his children. Why would he allow bad things to happen to those who are his dedicated followers?

A few years ago a visiting speaker in our church said with ironic emphasis, "If suffering is so wonderful, why don't you all come up here and pray that you might experience it?" His belief, apparently, was that if we suffer it is our own fault (lack of commitment, lack of faith) or perhaps even our own misguided choice.

I agree that suffering is awful. It also seems to be inevitable. The prophet says, "When you pass through the waters . . . When you walk through the flames . . ." The prophet's words seem to assume suffering as an unavoidable aspect of human experience.

Fire and flood are perhaps the two worst natural disasters, and they serve here also as metaphors for all those uncontrollable events which sweep over human life. The flames will come smoking and blazing; the flood will come with tremendous shock waves, carrying everything before it. I think of personal experiences with flood and fire. Several years ago the Thompson River in Colorado exploded through the valley. Cars, houses, even some large rocks were moved in the torrent. I recall also wheat field fires on the plains of Kansas where I grew up—great billowing clouds of black smoke visible for miles on the horizon, flames racing high in the dry air, popping, crackling sounds as the fire was driven forward by the south wind. Woe to any truck or combine in the harvest field that was caught in the path of the speeding inferno.

For humans, too, the floods and fire storms come. One of my sisters has for years had severe problems with her back. Surgery seemed to exacerbate her situation rather than relieve it. She could walk or lie down; sitting was impossible. Her husband was a Bible school principal, minister and evangelist, one who did a considerable amount of travelling in his work. For this they had bought a small R-V so my sister could also travel, lying on the cot.

Early one morning after a strenuous session at the Bible school, my brother-in-law fell asleep while driving, and the van hurtled down an embankment. My sister's back was broken in the accident, and for a time life itself hung in the balance. The two were joined in their prayers by their family and many other believers across the church. Eventually, after weeks of hospitalization and several surgeries, my sister returned home, a paraplegic who had much to relearn.

Both my sister and her husband were people of deep faith; both responded to the situation with grace and courage. Progress was difficult, the recovery slow, but months later my sister was able to accomplish more than one could have anticipated for a woman in her sixties recovering from such grievous injuries. And her loving, devoted husband cared for her better than most nurses could.

Prayers were not fully being answered as we had hoped, but my sister and husband were coping despite their greatly changed circumstances and curtailed activities. No longer would there be extended evangelistic trips across the eastern United States with my sister accompanying her husband; no longer could they open their home to large numbers of overnight guests. Yet living in a new house specially designed to accommodate a paraplegic's needs, they began to develop some semblance of reasonable order in their living routines. But the story isn't finished. My brother-in-law began to experience discomfort and then pain: eventually a doctor's diagnosis pronounced the dreaded word, *cancer*. After several months I preached his memorial sermon. It seemed impossible. He was always the strong one, never ill, always able to help others. He would, we assumed, always care for his wife.

I know of no one with a deeper faith in God, a more committed life of devotion to him. Yet to my sister's suffering—the flames and floods of continuing pain—was added loneliness.

Suffering is awful—and seemingly unavoidable.

Where is God When We Suffer?

The most incredible, gut-wrenching agony I have ever experienced was the loss of our daughter. Where was God when the tractor-trailer rig rear-ended several cars, then smashed over into the lane of oncoming traffic? Surely, it wouldn't have taken a large miracle for God to have stopped the rig on the median strip—or to have delayed Janelle's return home by a minute.

Where was God?

There seem to be several answers to this question which sounds so simple but which allows no easy solution. One response is that it's a matter of simple physics: the physical laws are set into action, and certain results can be expected. A tractor-trailer rig weighing so many tons, travelling at a certain rate of speed . . . calculate the answer. God watches, he observes from his position on the balcony of human affairs—he may even be sorry. But there is nothing God can do to stop the physically inevitable. No miracles will bail us out.

The advantage of this view is that God cannot be held responsible for what happens. You can't *blame* God if he doesn't control events. The disadvantage, of course, is that God seems fairly powerless and incapable of helping us.

A second position is almost the obverse of the former: in this view God regularly performs miracles for his people, if they have faith and call out to him. God is eager to help; if we don't avail ourselves of divine aid, that's our problem, not his. Various Scriptures are appealed to in support of this view:

"Ask and it will be given to you; seek and you will find; knock and the door will be opened to you. For everyone who asks receives; he who seeks finds; and to him who knocks, the door will be opened" (Matthew 7:7-8). Or again, "If you believe, you will receive whatever you ask for in prayer" (Matthew 21:22). The instances can be multiplied: "If you remain in me," Jesus said, "and my words remain in you, ask whatever you wish, and it will be given you" (John 15:7).

The advantage of this second view of God should be fairly obvious: he is the great rescuer, the deliverer who takes us through all the Red Seas of our lives. Nothing escapes God's notice; nothing is too large or small for God to do for his children.

The disadvantage, unfortunately, is that it doesn't seem to match our experience. Where was God when my mother prayed for seventeen long years for healing, and yet remained an invalid or semi-invalid for the rest of her life? Where was God when my sister and her husband cried out in their extremity?

A third view emphasizes God's sovereignty. God alone chooses when and how to act. Those holding the third position would see the second view as being too coercive, too demanding: we make of God a divine dispenser of candy bars, favors and special miracles to be handed out to all takers. No, say those arguing for God's sovereignty, the Lord God alone will choose to act—or not to act—as he pleases.

The advantage of this third view is that God is in control. Nothing ultimately happens outside divine providence. In the words of a song I sang as a child, "He's got the whole world in his hands." Or in the familiar words from Robert Browning's *Pippa Passes:* "God's in his heaven; all's right with the world."

The disadvantage of this view is God's apparent inconsistency. Why does he help sometimes, but at other times remain silent? Why does he reveal himself on occasion, but at other times hides himself? With the prophet one says, "Truly you are a God who hides himself, O God and Savior of Israel" (Isaiah 45:15).

Somehow it would seem simpler if God never intervened; then at least we could know what to expect. The laws of physics, the laws of cell growth—with these alone we would have to cope. On the other hand, if we could always expect him to bail us out of our floundering ship, that would be wonderful. But how can we make sense of this muddle, this divine inconsistency?

If God really is sovereign, why does he allow such awful things to occur? Gerald Oosterveen, whose young lad was dying of cancer, writes in *Too Early Frost*, "Occasionally someone would try to comfort or encourage us by reaffirming that God makes no mistakes, that nothing happens without his will, that all of this was part of some wonderful plan he has for our lives. For me, those assurances crumbled each time I stood beside my son's bed as he cried in his sleep or when I saw him walk across the lawn with that slight limp that was just becoming noticeable."

What is the meaning of justice—if God is truly sovereign? Why do people die untimely deaths? The Psalmist asked that question, "You have put me in the lowest pit, in the darkest depths.... You have taken from me my closest friends ... Do those who are dead rise up and praise you?" (Psalm 88).

Why is there no discernible pattern in life—and death? "Surely," the Psalmist cried out, "in vain have I kept my heart pure; in vain have I washed my hands in innocence" (Psalm 73:13). How unfair life seems! Janelle never caused her parents a moment's worry about her lifestyle. Never did we stay awake wondering about the company she was keeping. Her morals were impeccable. Yet she was ripped from us.

So how does one answer the questions of God's justice, his fairness, his involvement in the world? I believe in God's ultimate sovereignty—but that is not necessarily comforting to us humans in our finite dreams and aspirations. Philip Yancey puts the matter well in *Disappointment with God:* "I have had to conclude that divine sovereignty means at least this: only God can determine what is of value to God."

I come then, finally, somewhat reluctantly, to a fourth position, a position which does not greatly cheer me: God resides in *mystery*; he will not easily be defined. "I am who I am"—that was his word to Moses. He is self-existent; he doesn't need to depend on anyone else. God is beyond our categories, our definitions, our causal logic. "I am who I am."

But we Christians in the West have the need to understand, to explain, to rationalize. One explanation for Janelle's accident, an explanation first made to us by a kind bishop in the church, was that Janelle's sudden death affected many people. Perhaps she will now, through her dying, do more for others than had she lived. This reasoning, though well-intentioned, seems specious to me. How quickly the shock wears off for all but those family and friends intimately involved with the situation. On the other hand, had Janelle lived, she would surely have touched at least a hundred people (two hundred people?) each year—in the hospital, in the classroom. Multiply those people by almost fifty years of service, and I find the mathematics irrefutable.

Another explanation, offered in several guises, was that God in his sovereignty was purging us. "Whom the Lord loveth he chasteneth." The argument is hardly new or original: that's what Job's friends thought, too. As Nicholas Wolterstorff puts it in *Lament for a Son*, the friends argued: "God did it, Job; he was the agent of your children's death. He did it because of some wickedness in you; he did it to punish you. Nothing indeed in your public life would seem to merit such retribution; it must then be something in your private inner life." But, says Wolterstorff, "The writer of Job refuses to say that God views the lives and deaths of children as cats-o'-nine-tails with which to lacerate parents."

How, then, shall we explain? I have been forced to say that even as I can't explain God, I can't understand the circumstances in which we find ourselves. And while I affirm God's sovereignty, I am not immediately encouraged by it. But in the midst of our perplexities we make choices. As C. S. Lewis says, "You bid for God or no God, for a good God or the cosmic sadist, for eternal life or non-entity."

On the Sunday following the accident, the following verse by a Holocaust victim was printed on the church bulletin cover:

I believe in the sun
    even when it does not shine;
I believe in love
    even when it is not shown;
I believe in God
    even when he does not speak.

You make choices, and then you live by those choices. Job, who had lost possessions, health and not one child—but all—said, "Though he slay me, yet will I trust him." Despite this ringing affirmation, Job later became increasingly distressed with the injustice of life and the continued questioning of his friends.

Finally, God revealed himself in power and spoke in a mighty storm. God asked Job varied and puzzling questions about the mysteries and powers of nature, questions which Job couldn't answer. Job listened and then acknowledged, "I know that you can do all things; no plan of yours can be thwarted." Furthermore, he said, my knowledge of you had been indirect, "but now my eyes have seen you. Therefore I despise myself and repent in dust and ashes" (Job 42:2, 4-5).

The first time I carefully read the book of Job was in a world literature class in college. I still recall the sense of outrage which I felt at the conclusion of the "debate" with God. What kind of answer is this? It's a non sequitur—it doesn't fit the problem. Job had been asking for justice—he was shown power. Eventually, I have come to accept that we must rest without answers, that if there is an answer it is that we cannot fully know God's way.

As God told Moses, "My face you cannot see and live." Pascal says rather enigmatically, "A religion which does not affirm that God is hidden is not true—truly you are a hidden God." I rest, then, in a God who is beyond our understanding, a God whose mystery I cannot fathom, a God whose ways I cannot always justify. But I also believe that God does not abandon us in our pain.

Why Does God Suffer?

A curious question, surely, for how could the omnipotent

God of the universe, the Creator and Sustainer of all things, the Alpha and the Omega, how could this God *suffer?*

The mystery is that God was in Christ reconciling the world to himself. The mystery is that in the crucified Christ, God shares our pain, our anguished cries of heartache, our unspeakable agony of spirit. He wakes with us in our sleepless hours; he sits with us in our loneliness and wretchedness. "When you pass through the waters, I will be with you. . . . When you walk though the fire you will not be burned."

The prophet says in words familiar to many, "Surely he hath borne our griefs and carried our sorrows." In the past I interpreted his word as a metaphoric statement of God's care. Now I read it more literally: our sorrows have become God's. In Jesus' dark night of the soul, he cried, "My soul is exceedingly sorrowful even unto death."

With great power Wolterstorff writes,

> How is faith to endure, O God, when you allow all this scraping and tearing on us? You have allowed rivers of blood to flow, mountains of suffering to pile up, sobs to become humanity's song—all without lifting a finger that we could see. You have allowed bonds of love beyond number to be painfully snapped. If you have not abandoned us, explain yourself.
>
> We strain to hear. But instead of hearing an answer we catch sight of God himself scraped and torn. Through our tears we see the tears of God.

This, then, is the mystery: that the omnipotent God in some unfathomable ways suffers with us. When Daniel's three friends were thrown into the explosively hot incinerator, the king expected them to collapse in a moment. No one could survive the fierce heat. But their *ropes* were burned off—not their flesh.

And Nebuchadnezzar, the king, politician and realist, asks in astonishment, Didn't we throw three men into the furnace? Yes, of course, his advisors respond. "Look," he says, "I see four men walking around in the fire, unbound and unharmed, and the fourth looks like a son of the gods."

I still have no satisfactory answers to the questions of suffering. But I rest in the assurance that the fourth man will walk through the flames with us. Our dark night of the soul has become his.

In Henri Nouwen's marvelous little book *The Wounded Healer,* he writes of the Master, the Wounded Healer:

> The master is coming—not tomorrow,
> but today,
> not next year, but this year,
> not after all our misery is passed,
> but in the middle of it,
> not in another place
> but right here where we are standing.

Through fire and flood we have the assurance that the Wounded Healer stands with us in the blistering flames and the smashing torrent. He has not abandoned us. Amen.

12.

Hope in Christ

Behold, I will create
    new heavens and a new earth.
The former things will not be remembered,
    nor will they come to mind.
But be glad and rejoice forever
      in what I will create,
for I will create Jerusalem to be a delight
    and its people a joy.
Never again will there be in it
    an infant that lives but a few days,
    or an old man who does not live out his years;
he who dies at a hundred
    will be thought a mere youth.
        —Isaiah 65:17-20

If in this life only we have hope
in Christ, we are of all men
most miserable.
        —I Corinthians 15:19 KJV

In a flash, at a trumpet crash,
I am all at once what Christ is, since he was what I am, and
This Jack, joke, poor potsherd, patch, matchwood,
        immortal diamond,
    Is immortal diamond.
                    —*Gerard Manley Hopkins, "That Nature Is a*
                    Heraclitean Fire and of the Comfort of the Resurrection"

The death of someone close to us brings with unprece-
dented urgency and power the question, "After death, what
then?" Is there, in fact, anything beyond this life with its joys
and sadnesses, its triumphs and failures, its hopes and fears?
Is there something more, or do we sink into oblivion, remembered briefly by those who knew us, longer by those who
loved us—and then BLANKNESS? We exist for a time in
memories, yes, but is there something beyond?

The ancient Hebrews had little concept of immortality. In
now familiar words we hear the sighing of the Psalmist: "As
for man, his days are as grass: as a flower of the field, so he
flourisheth. For the wind passeth over it, and it is gone; and
the place thereof shall know it no more" (Psalm 103:15-16
KJV). I think of my mother and father, my brother-in-law,
and my father-in-law who died after a thirty-year-long struggle
with Parkinson's disease—and now my only daughter, cut off
in the April of her life. Do they become as broken, brown
grass or wilted, blackened flowers? Is this the end?

Or to choose another view, are the ancient Greeks correct
in their belief in immortality, but an immortality of spirit
living in an idealized form, without bodily existence? Perhaps, then, Janelle's spirit is alive in some evanescent, shad-
owy realm? Has her spirit been merged with a transcendent

ALL?

We humans, who can remember the past and anticipate the future, seem to have a deep-seated urgency to know something of a life beyond this present life. In the simple words of the gospel song,

> This world is not my home.
> I'm just a passing through.
>
> ♦ ♦ ♦
>
> If heaven's not my home,
> Then, Lord, what will I do?

In his profound word of longing, the Apostle Paul writes, "I consider that our present sufferings are not worth comparing with the glory that will be revealed in us. . . . the creation itself will be liberated from its bondage to decay and brought into the glorious freedom of the children of God" (Romans 8:18,21).

Throughout the New Testament we find strong reasons to hope for a new order of creation, a fresh beginning that will in some yet unfathomed way be our home. There remains, however, an essential mystery, and Scriptures do not provide complete answers to all our questions about this "New Jerusalem," nor about our personal existence in it.

Even before Janelle's death I had at various times reflected upon the departed dead, particularly my parents, and about the abode of the dead. Now I think with more eagerness about heaven and with greater tentativeness about earthly existence. While I still enjoy the crispness of a bright October morning in Pennsylvania or the splendor of a June sun setting over a Kansas wheat field, I think more about another country, another life. After the death of a child, I have found that there is a turning loose, a letting go, which I would never have anticipated. Life on earth still has its richness, its pleasures, its deep joys, but something has been lost. The old zest can never be quite recovered.

The point came forcefully home to me some time ago in a dream. All of us were at home, in bed, and the boys were playing some music rather too loudly for Janelle's taste. She said she couldn't sleep with so much noise, and then she herself began singing very loudly and with much pain in her voice:

> Somewhere there is a land
> Where dreams come true,
> Where skies are ever bright and blue,
> The dreams I cherish here
> Will be complete up there
> In that happy land
> Where dreams come true.

I awoke with a start, considerable anguish in my own heart. Then I thought that perhaps this is a special word to me: Janelle is in a land where she no longer needs to strive so hard for perfection, where her growth will occur without the anguish she often experienced on earth.

Because of our frame of reference we often tend to envision heaven as a land, a place, but surely this new kingdom exists outside our current categories of space. As David Ewert says in *And Then Comes the End*, "It should be said immediately that heaven cannot be located in the cosmic order as we know it . . . Heaven is where God is. He was there long before he 'created the heavens and the earth,' and he will be there when this heaven and earth pass away."

But if heaven is where God is, how do we move from our present realm of existence to this new sphere? A major theme in Scripture seems to be *transformation*. The Apostle Paul speaks in an analogy of the "dying" of a grain of wheat as it is sowed, and then becomes a new plant, lush and growing, linked genetically with the seed, but transformed into new life. Likewise, the Apostle argues, the resurrected body will be transformed as it is changed from its earthly form to its heavenly one. How the body is changed remains part of the mystery of the resurrection.

But one may ask—as I have often asked—what happens between the time of the death of a person and the resurrection of the dead? I continue to wonder—how much does Janelle know about us, about my writing of this lament, for example. Does she realize the strong memories that each Friday afternoon brings to me? Obviously, the departed ones do not have omniscient knowledge. But, on the other hand, they must know more perfectly than we. No longer do they see through a glass darkly, but they know even as they are known. Does that knowledge include awareness of us who remain—and who continue to love?

And in what "form" do the departed dead remain? Is Janelle a disembodied *spirit*, alive and conscious, waiting with Jesus for the resurrection of the body? Or is she "asleep" in Jesus, in a kind of limbo, awaiting the resurrection from the dead? Or can it be, as Norman Anderson suggests, "When we die, we pass out of a space-time continuum into a realm where time is merged in eternity; so might it not be that those who die in Christ are immediately with him, in their resurrection bodies?" That is, while the resurrection is *future* for us, could it not be *present* for those who have passed beyond our constraints of time? Has the transformation *already* taken place for them? I am personally inclined toward this third view, though I grew up accepting the first.

Dreams are no proof of anything, of course, but I was most comforted some months ago when I saw Janelle in heaven. I asked her whether she had seen Grandmommy (my mother) and the others in the family. "Oh, yes," she replied, "but I saw Jesus first."

In my dream I didn't "see" heaven, though I was conscious of her presence there. The apocalypse of John pictures heaven with streets of gold, marvelous jewels, gates of pearl. But many today find that view not too attractive. A graduate school professor of mine, an agnostic, said that he found the usual concepts of heaven about as exciting as dirty dish water. One clarification should be obvious: the Apostle John was limited to human language, as we all are, and he was attempting to communicate (among other things) the *glory* of heaven.

More important than any specific "physical" details of heaven is the sense that this is a new order of creation. Most significantly, *God* is in heaven in all his majestic holiness, his indescribable splendor. "See, the home of God is among mortals. He will dwell with them as their God; they will be his peoples, and God himself will be with them" (Revelation 21:3 NRSV).

When my brother-in-law lay dying of cancer in 1983, he suddenly sat up in bed, his face transformed. "What do you see?" his family asked him.

"I see Jesus," he said clearly. Then with a voice preternaturally strong, he sang, "Blessed assurance, Jesus is mine. Oh, what a foretaste of glory divine." Soon afterward he lapsed into a coma. Whatever one makes of my brother-in-law's vision, the Revelation of John makes clear that heaven is preeminently where *God* is.

And if God is there, heaven is a place of fruitfulness, creativity, wholeness, light and life. Especially life. For the old enemy death will be finally defeated: "Never again," says the prophet, "will there be in it an infant that lives but a few days, or an old man who does not live out his years"—or, one might add—a twenty-one-year-old crushed in the blossom of early spring.

In this heaven of God we will have, I believe, a conscious, personal existence. To the thief on the cross, Jesus gave this promise, "Today you will be with me in Paradise," a promise, I think, of continuing personal existence. And this existence will be with God. Being in heaven means living with God in transformed openness. "They will see his [God's] face, and his name will be on their foreheads" (Revelation 22:4). In our jadedness we may not be stunned by this word, but when the greatest prophet who ever lived, Moses, asked to see God's glory, even he was given only a special glimpse.

Janelle, you live in the light of God's presence. Were we to see at close range the light of the sun, we would be blinded, yet we see the twinkling of stars that give us hints of the vast galaxies which lie beyond. We who remain are yet in the kindergarten of our knowledge; we know enough to encourage us, to give us hope in Christ, but not enough to make us proud or boastful.

The Apostle Paul, speaking of himself, said that he knew a

man who "was caught up into Paradise. He heard inexpressible things, things that man is not permitted to tell" (II Corinthians 12:4). You, too, my beloved daughter, have been caught up into Paradise. Through our misty lenses we strain to see you. We cannot yet hear what you would tell us.

13.

Living in Eternity
—and in Time

We are not endowed with real life, and all that seems
most real about us is but the thinnest substance of a
dream—till the heart be touched. That touch creates us.
—*Nathaniel Hawthorne, Notebooks*

He sees that they are the dead, and they are alive. He
sees that he lives in eternity as he lives in time, and
nothing is lost.
—*Wendell Berry, Remembering*

"Never the less let my pardon be,
My pearl," said I, "though I questions pose.
I should not test thy wit so fine
Who to Christ's chamber are elect.
I am but mingled with muck and mold,
And thou so rich a perfect rose
And abidest here near this blissful bank,
Where joy of life may never die."
—*The Pearl, a fourteenth-century lament for a daughter*

This summer I returned to the simple country graveyard where my parents—and many others whom I have known from my home community in Kansas—lie buried. The five year's growth of turf on Dad's grave still includes some weeds, but after seventeen years the grass on Mom's grave blends naturally, completely with the surrounding sod. I have come to journey back in time, to remember, to refuse to forget. I study the simple headstone with its engraved wheat straw. How little this sturdy, unpretentious stone reveals about their dreams and aspirations, their successes and their sicknesses, their loyalties and their loneliness.

I step over to visit my sister Matilda's burial site and try to imagine whom this eleven-year-old Nisly whom I never saw might resemble. No pictures remain of this my oldest sister, so I can only surmise that she had the high forehead and the bright blue eyes characteristic of other siblings. As I think of my sister, I inevitably think of another oldest daughter, my daughter, who for years has accompanied me on this annual path to our ancestors. This year I have come alone.

I think of my mother and how she would grieve at each *Jahrzeit*, each anniversary, of Matilda's death. My dad never spoke much about his firstborn daughter, whom he lost in her preadolescence. His response to the pain seemed to be to shut the door rather firmly on the past. He was a sensitive, caring man; I'm sure his response did not mean that he didn't suffer. I wish I could talk to him now since we share fully in the fraternity of sorrow. I wish I could ask him how he coped in silence. Would he approve my public lament?

A few steps further and I see the memorial stone for a young nephew, a namesake, and the single plot for infant twins, a niece and nephew (also my namesake). In the corner

I see the memorial for fifteen infants and young children whose graves were moved from a failed community in western Kansas. I think of all the grief which these families endured—no doubt silently and stoically as good Germanic people often would—but with powerful feelings of loss, nonetheless.

Moving back to the old rusty iron gate at the entrance, I stop to read the inscription for my ancestor Abraham, who died over a century ago. I think of my father who was named for this grandfather and wonder why I didn't carry on the ancestral name.

The sky is a brilliant June blue, there is not even enough breeze to blow away the mosquitoes, and I am both in time and outside time. In the words of Wendell Berry, "Now they come to him again, those who have brought him here and who remain—not in memory, but near to memory, in the place itself and in his flesh, ready always to be remembered—so that the place, the present life of it, resonates within time and within times, as it could not do if time were all that it is living in."

"In the place itself and in his flesh"—a powerful word for remembering, since memories often lie so deep that words seem incapable of rendering them with accuracy or adequacy. One is left with the searing realization that the attempt to communicate felt experience at this deep level is at best an approximation, an attempt to move from being isolated to the potential for mutually comprehending. And always communication at that level remains a goal, never a complete achievement.

Perhaps only those entering death's other kingdom understand clearly. Last fall, a year after the accident, a much loved bishop in the church preached his final series of renewal meetings. For forty-seven years a minister, for many years a mission board president, a devoted husband and family man, one who never smoked nor drank, Bishop Raymond Charles was suffering with the serpent cancer in his liver.

Although he felt physically upset and nauseated, Bishop Charles preached with deep genuineness and honesty from his wealth of experience. He admitted to having more questions than answers to the problem of suffering, but his integrity, his courage and his warm caring powerfully modeled for us his faith in Christ.

On Saturday night at the end of the service, too weak to stand to greet people, he sat at the back, large drops of sweat gathering on his forehead. Considerably moved at his embodiment of the faith, I leaned down and said, "I think you will see our daughter before we do." He smiled warmly and even in his weakness firmly pressed my hand.

Speaking of his present and future residence, he said, "I live in Christ, and I live in the body of Christ (the church)." He refused to blame God nor did he attempt to explain the sickness which had been his companion for the last five years. With the poet-priest Gerard Manley Hopkins he could have said, "Thou [God] art lightning and love, I found it, a winter and warm." God is both threatening cold and welcoming warmth.

A few weeks after the weekend series, Bishop Charles saw God in a fuller dimension than any earthlings, "mingled with muck and mold," ever can. But before he left, he stood on the border and gave us glimpses of that other kingdom.

A few weeks before that renewal series, our family quietly honored Janelle's birthday. A single velvety red rose and a flickering white candle in her nursing lamp: these simple beauties helped us reflect on the loveliness of our daughter's life. And I thought of the thrill and mystery of her birth—and pondered again the awful moment of her anti-birth, a terrible crushing—a time so unlike the natural pressure when she was pressed through her mother's birth canal on that November dawn twenty-two years earlier.

Remembering her birthday, one of Janelle's good friends thoughtfully sent a card which read, "May you find comfort in knowing that those who love God live forever in Heaven, as their memory lives on earth in the hearts of those who love them." Both aspects, the heavenly and the earthly, do offer comfort.

On the first *Jahrzeit* of the accident we received a beautiful, personally designed card from a secretary, lovely roses from a colleague, notes from others. Two young women tramped a half mile through the rain to bring us flowers on this occasion. To know that one is not forgotten is a gracious blessing, a heartening encouragement.

Several students, and former students, could not have been more supportive. A few have become "daughters" in a rather remarkable way. One brought us a lovely cross-stitched plaque which she had designed and stitched for us. Others stop by the office to chat, to cry, to offer encouragement. I doubt whether they can fully understand what a godsend, what a rare and special gift, their love and care have been.

There are other providential gifts for which I have even less explanation, but for which I offer heartfelt thanks. During one Sunday afternoon's nap, I dreamed that I called Janelle on the phone, and we had a long conversation. When Laura heard about the call, she was disappointed and asked whether that meant she couldn't talk. "Oh, no," I responded, "you call and talk to her as long as you want."

On another occasion I had been praying for some time that I might again see Janelle in a dream. Perhaps like the father in *The Pearl* I was granted a vision of my daughter. I saw her very clearly, and the first word she said was, "I must have looked terrible [in the coffin] with my nose all smashed up." "No," I told her, "you looked beautiful." And I meant it with all my heart.

Always Janelle appeared beautiful in my dreams. Once I dreamed that she had just returned from a cross-cultural study trip abroad. I was thrilled to see her again, and as she approached, I exclaimed, "You look beautiful," and hugged and kissed her.

"Oh, you men all say the same thing," she said in a teasing tone, brown eyes laughing at me. It was a restorative moment.

No doubt there may be psychological explanations for these dreams. I accept them as part of the divine ministry of comfort. For the most part, comfort has been mediated through people, through shared tears, acts of kindness, words of encouragement, the healing touch—all rare gifts of grace. But I am also thankful for these "visitations" which I cannot fully understand nor adequately explain.

Finally, I accept that the time-bound cannot fathom the timeless, that the finite must bow before the infinite, that words must lapse into silence. John Leax, poet and believer, a man from whom I have learned much, writes in his long poem, "The Geography of Love":

> There is no turn
> we can't by grace negotiate.
>
> We have come to this place by choice.

We have crawled like cicadas
from the years of darkness,
split our backs by will,
and left the old nature
fastened to the tree.

Yet, we will fall into the ground.
The grave, too, is Christ's.
It is his place.

Eternity is now.
What we are is what
we will become,
and what we are is here.

In the geography of love
the only place is Christ.
We dwell in him,
the present of the Father.

I still believe in God the Father Almighty, maker of heaven
and earth. I believe in the resurrection of the body, and the
life everlasting. But I confess that, for now, I see through a
glass, darkly, waiting in hope until I can see face to face.

About the Author

Paul W. Nisly was born in southcentral Kansas where he spent the first 23 years of his life. He attended Hesston College in Kansas and then was graduated from Eastern Mennonite College with a degree in English. He completed the Ph.D. in English at the University of Kansas.

For the last 20 years, he has been a professor of English at Messiah College in Pennsylvania and has chaired the Department of Language, Literature and Fine Arts.

He says that teaching, writing and preaching have been richly rewarding aspects of his life. Nothing has been more important, however, than the deep joy he and his wife Laura have experienced in being the parents of three children.